DIGGING UP THE PAST

THE TITANIC

BY EMILY ROSE OACHS

BELLWETHER MEDIA • MINNEAPOLIS, MN

TM

Are you ready to take it to the extreme? Torque books thrust you into the action-packed world of sports, vehicles, mystery, and adventure. These books may include dirt, smoke, fire, and chilling tales. **WARNING**: read at your own risk.

This edition first published in 2020 by Bellwether Media, Inc.

No part of this publication may be reproduced in whole or in part without written permission of the publisher. For information regarding permission, write to Bellwether Media, Inc., Attention: Permissions Department, 6012 Blue Circle Drive, Minnetonka, MN 55343.

Library of Congress Cataloging-in-Publication Data

Names: Oachs, Emily Rose, author.
Title: The Titanic / by Emily Rose Oachs.
Description: Minneapolis, MN : Bellwether Media, Inc., [2020] | Series:
   Torque: Digging Up the Past | Audience: Ages: 7-12. | Includes
   bibliographical references and index.
Identifiers: LCCN 2018060233 (print) | LCCN 2019000283 (ebook) |
   ISBN 9781618916433 (ebook) | ISBN 9781644870716 (hardcover :
   alk. paper)
Subjects: LCSH: Titanic (Steamship)–Juvenile literature. | Shipwrecks–North
   Atlantic Ocean–Juvenile literature.
Classification: LCC G530.T6 (ebook) | LCC G530.T6 O33 2020 (print)
   | DDC 910.9163/4–dc23
LC record available at https://lccn.loc.gov/2018060233

Editor: Betsy Rathburn   Designer: Brittany McIntosh

Printed in the United States of America, North Mankato, MN.

TABLE OF CONTENTS

RELIVING THE TRAGEDY

You enter a museum about the *Titanic*. Each room tells a different part of the famous shipwreck's story. Survivor stories show the fear and bravery of passengers as they escaped the sinking ship.

Underwater video shows the *Titanic* as it lies today. The rusted ship looks ghostly in its watery grave. What other stories does it have to tell?

WHAT IS THE *TITANIC?*

The *Titanic* was a **luxury** passenger ship built in 1912. It was among the largest and fastest ships in the ocean! Many people believed it was unsinkable.

WHAT WAS THE *TITANIC'S* ROUTE?

Southampton

New York City

Titanic wreck

PASSENGER CLASSES

Passengers aboard the *Titanic* were grouped into three classes. First- and second-class passengers were wealthy. They had the best rooms. Third-class passengers had cheaper tickets. Their rooms were far below deck!

On April 10, 1912, the *Titanic* set out on its **maiden voyage**. It was traveling to New York City from Southampton, England. Around 2,200 people were on board.

iceberg

Four days into the journey, nearby ships reported **icebergs**. The crew was on the lookout for any in the *Titanic's* path.

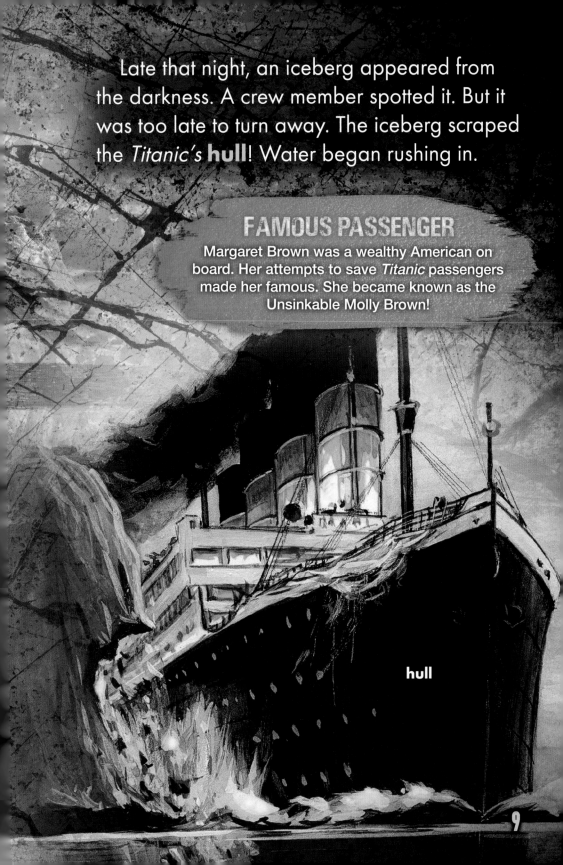

Late that night, an iceberg appeared from the darkness. A crew member spotted it. But it was too late to turn away. The iceberg scraped the *Titanic's* **hull**! Water began rushing in.

FAMOUS PASSENGER

Margaret Brown was a wealthy American on board. Her attempts to save *Titanic* passengers made her famous. She became known as the Unsinkable Molly Brown!

hull

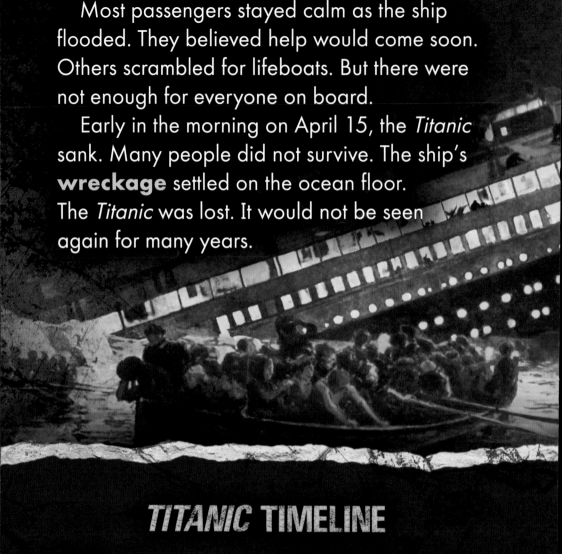

Most passengers stayed calm as the ship flooded. They believed help would come soon. Others scrambled for lifeboats. But there were not enough for everyone on board.

Early in the morning on April 15, the *Titanic* sank. Many people did not survive. The ship's **wreckage** settled on the ocean floor. The *Titanic* was lost. It would not be seen again for many years.

TITANIC TIMELINE

1909:
Construction on the RMS *Titanic* begins in Belfast, Ireland

April 14, 1912:
The *Titanic* strikes an iceberg late at night

April 10, 1912:
The *Titanic* sets out from Southampton, England, to begin its maiden voyage

April 15, 1912:
The *Titanic* sinks in the early morning

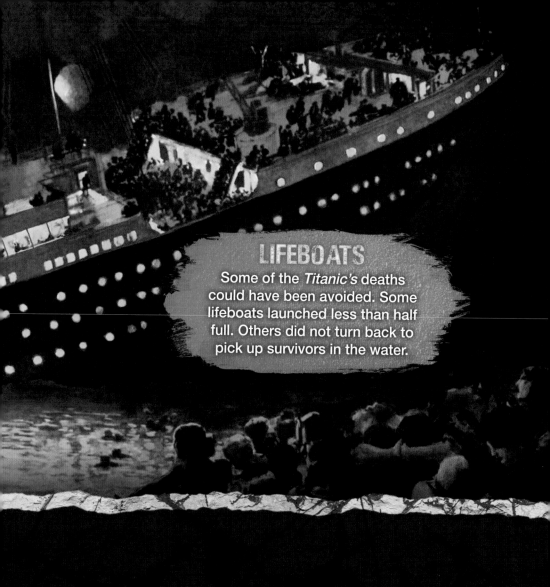

LIFEBOATS

Some of the *Titanic's* deaths could have been avoided. Some lifeboats launched less than half full. Others did not turn back to pick up survivors in the water.

1977:
Robert Ballard leads his first expedition to search for the *Titanic*

2012:
The *Titanic* wreck becomes protected under UNESCO rules on the 100th anniversary of its sinking

1985:
Ballard and his team discover the remains of the *Titanic* on the ocean floor

A HUGE DISCOVERY

Robert
Ballard

In 1985, **oceanographer** Robert Ballard went looking for the *Titanic*. Ballard's research ship towed cameras deep underwater. They sent images of the ocean floor back to the ship.

The cameras soon spotted something exciting. Ballard and his crew recognized a part of the *Titanic*. After 73 years, the *Titanic* had been found!

THE FINAL RESTING PLACE

The *Titanic* wreckage is 2.5 miles (4 kilometers) below the ocean's surface!

photo of the *Titanic* taken by Ballard's crew

Ballard soon found the ship's **bow**. It was still in excellent shape. The *Titanic's* **stern** rested about 2,000 feet (600 meters) away. It had suffered serious damage when it crashed to the ocean floor.

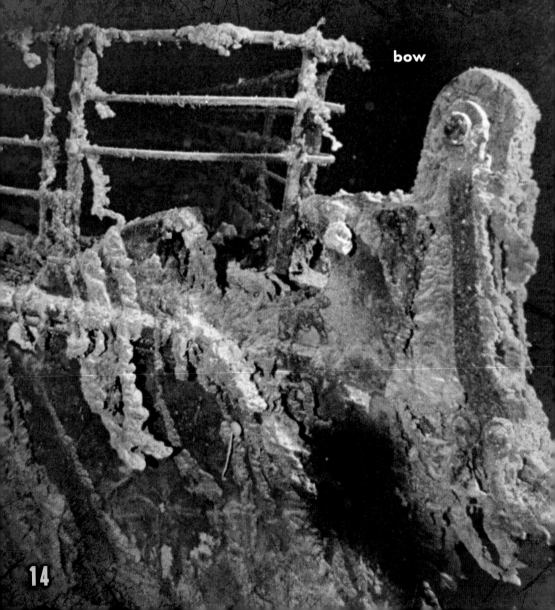

bow

The distance between bow and stern answered some questions. It **confirmed** what some survivors had described. The *Titanic* broke in half as it sank.

Experts have made many exciting finds near the *Titanic*. Some captured images of the ship's famous grand staircase. Another found the captain's own bathtub!

Thousands of items from the ship surrounded the wreck. Clothing and toys were easily spotted. Kitchen tools and dishes had also settled nearby.

The items created a large **debris field** around the ship. The field formed when items spilled from the ship's broken halves. It stretched for miles in every direction!

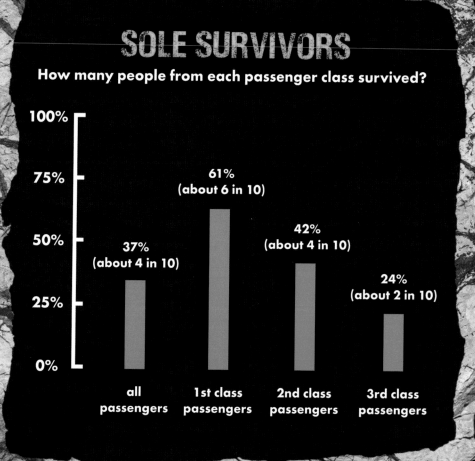

SOLE SURVIVORS

How many people from each passenger class survived?

- 100%
- 75% — 61% (about 6 in 10)
- 50% — 37% (about 4 in 10) — 42% (about 4 in 10)
- 25% — 24% (about 2 in 10)
- 0%

all passengers | 1st class passengers | 2nd class passengers | 3rd class passengers

UNDERWATER GRAVESITE

Since 1985, many explorers have visited the *Titanic*. Underwater robots help them see inside the ship. Some have collected **artifacts**.

Titanic artifact

exploring
the *Titanic*

People argue about gathering artifacts from
the *Titanic*. Some believe it **preserves** the
Titanic's history. But others point out that the
ship is a gravesite. It should be left in peace
to respect the dead. Still, many companies
continue to explore the site.

DISCOVERED IN RUST

Discovery: Rusty buildup on the *Titanic* shipwreck is caused by never-before-seen bacteria *Halomonas titanicae*

Date of Discovery: 2010

Process:

1. Used underwater robots to collect samples of icicle-like buildup called rusticles from the ship
2. Analyzed rusticles to determine what they are made of
3. Discovered rusticles contain bacteria, fungi, sand, shells, and other objects

What It Means:

- The Titanic may be gone by 2030 because of bacteria
- The bacteria may be used to break down harmful shipwrecks
- Knowledge of bacteria can help preserve other metal items underwater

The year 2012 marked 100 years since the *Titanic* sank. This brought new protections to the shipwreck. A **UNESCO** rule now protects it from human harm.

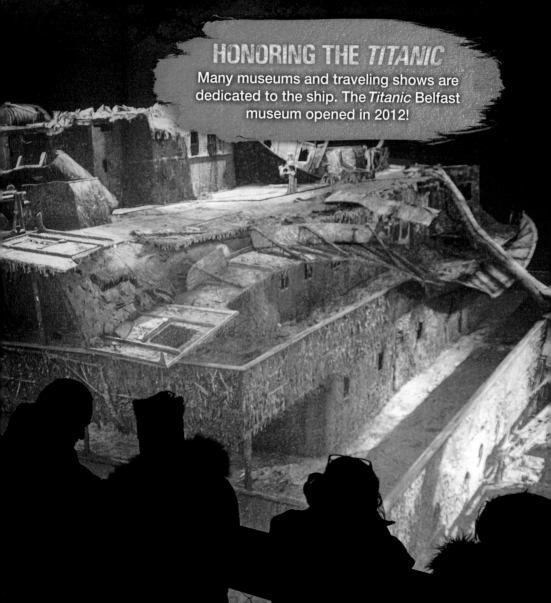

Still, experts believe the ship is in danger. It is naturally breaking down in the ocean. Someday, it may completely disappear. But the *Titanic's* **tragic** story will never fade from memory.

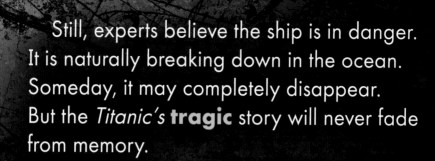

HONORING THE *TITANIC*

Many museums and traveling shows are dedicated to the ship. The *Titanic* Belfast museum opened in 2012!

GLOSSARY

artifacts—objects that save the history and culture of a past event or place

bow—the front end of a ship

confirmed—proved

debris field—a large area over which the remains of a disaster are scattered

hull—the body of a ship

icebergs—large pieces of ice floating in the ocean

luxury—expensive and offering great comfort

maiden voyage—the first trip a ship makes

oceanographer—a scientist who studies the ocean

preserves—protects

stern—the back end of a ship

tragic—sad or awful

UNESCO—a worldwide organization that works to protect important pieces of culture; UNESCO stands for United Nations Educational, Scientific, and Cultural Organization.

wreckage—the broken or destroyed remains of an object

TO LEARN MORE

AT THE LIBRARY

Burgan, Michael. *Finding the Titanic: How Images from the Ocean Depths Fueled Interest in the Doomed Ship.* North Mankato, Minn.: Compass Point Books, 2018.

Dougherty, Terri. *The Search for the Titanic: Finding the Ship's Watery Grave.* North Mankato, Minn.: Capstone Press, 2015.

Sabol, Stephanie. *What Was the Titanic?* New York, N.Y.: Penguin Workshop, 2018.

ON THE WEB

FACTSURFER

Factsurfer.com gives you a safe, fun way to find more information.

1. Go to www.factsurfer.com.

2. Enter "Titanic" into the search box and click Q.

3. Select your book cover to see a list of related web sites.

INDEX